ABC
of Australian Animals

Irene Morcombe

Aa Antechinus

The Brown Antechinus is a tiny marsupial that lives in the Australian forests and hunts at night. It prefers damp areas of the forest floor, where it digs for spiders and beetles among the leaf mulch and tree litter. During the day, it sleeps in a grass nest inside a hollow log, where it is dry and safe. When Antechinus babies are born, they crawl through the hairs of the mother's stomach and cling to her nipples. The mother carries her babies for approximately eight weeks.

Bb Bandicoot

The Barred Bandicoot, so named because of the faint stripes on its hindquarters, used to be found across most of Australia. But today this native marsupial can be seen in only a few safe places – mostly islands – where there are no sheep to destroy its habitat, and no cats and foxes to eat it. The Barred Bandicoot sleeps all day in a cosy nest of sticks and grass which is carefully hidden beneath a low growing shrub. After dark, it comes out to search for little insects and seeds.

Cuscus

The Spotted Cuscus is a treetop animal that lives in the Australian rainforests. During the day it hides among the big leaves of the Staghorn and Birds Nest ferns that grow high up on the trunks of the rainforest trees. At night it climbs about the treetops with the aid of a long curly tail, which it wraps firmly around the branches. It feeds on a diet of tender leaves.

Dd Dingo

The Dingo was brought to Australia by Indigenous Australians several thousand years ago as a domestic dog. It is the only wild dog in Australia, and although found in many parts of the country, it is rarely seen in areas where there are lots of people. Dingoes do not bark, but make a yelping, howling noise. They eat mainly rodents and rabbits, but also kill sheep. Dingoes mate for life. The female gives birth to a litter of three to four pups.

Ee

Emu

The Emu is the second largest bird in the world. It cannot fly but runs at speeds of up to 50 kilometres per hour. It is found in most areas of Australia. After the female Emu has laid up to eleven eggs, the male sits on a rough nest of sticks and grass and waits for the young to hatch. The male looks after the chicks for almost a year. Emus feed on insects, seeds and fruit. They particularly like the fruit of the Quandong tree.

Echidna

Echidnas are reptilian-like mammals which lay eggs. The female Echidna carries her egg in a pouch and when it is hatched, she suckles her baby on milk that seeps from her stomach. Echidnas roam throughout Australia. They eat ants and termites with their long sticky tongues. Their bodies are covered with sharp spines. When disturbed they burrow into the dirt with their strong claws, or roll into a ball to protect themselves.

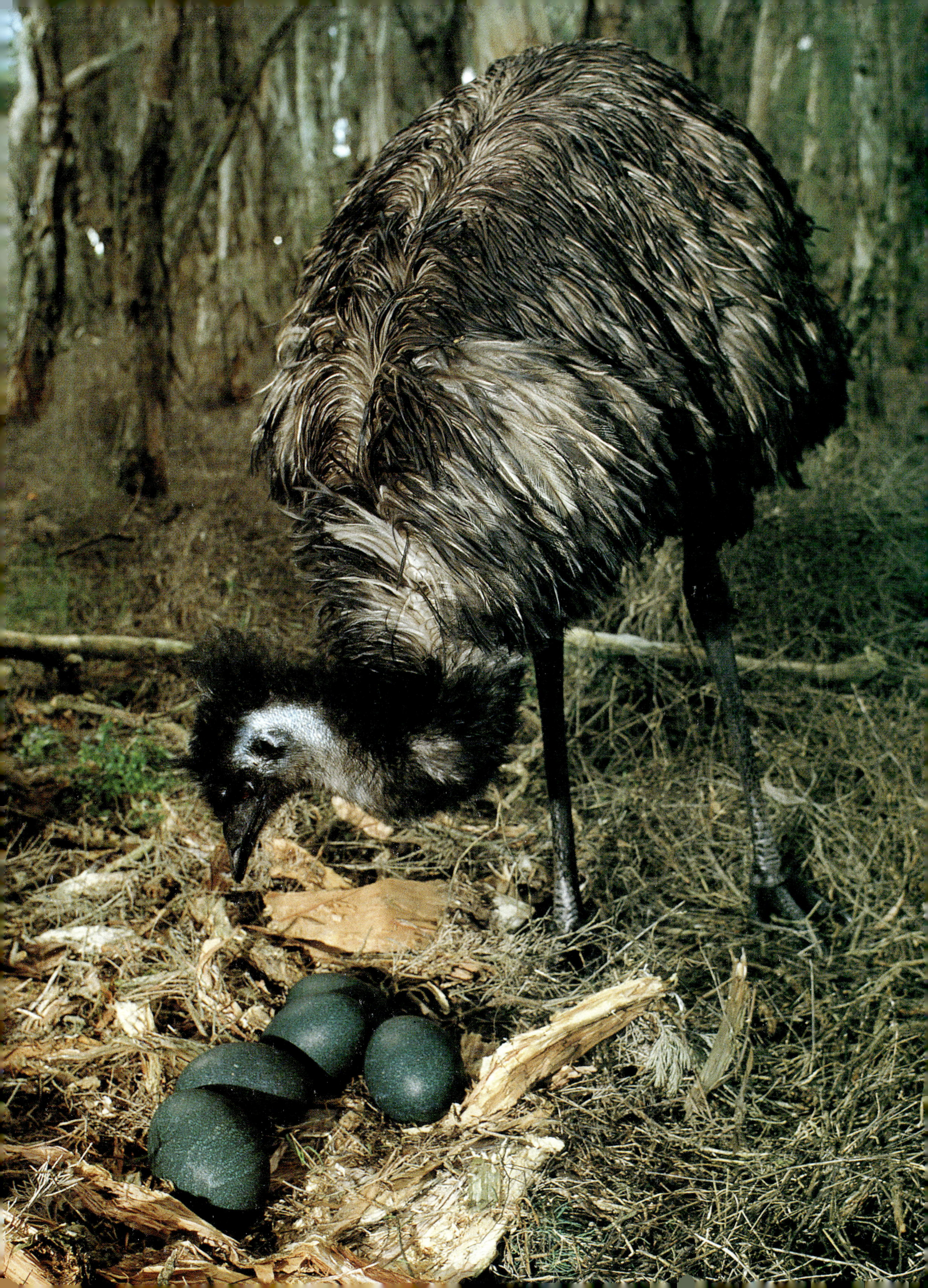

Ff Frog

The Giant Tree Frog is found in the rainforests of north Queensland. Being an amphibian, it lives on both land and water, and can be found near swamps and ponds, and under the moist leaves of the forest floor. Like most frogs, the Giant Tree Frog is active at night, when it searches for insects to eat. It lays its eggs in the water, which hatch into tiny tadpoles and develop into frogs.

Gg

Galah

The Galah is one of the best known Australian birds, and is found in most areas of Australia except dense forests. Galahs are usually seen in large noisy flocks. Their loud screeching is often accompanied by a range of antics, which includes raising their crests, lifting their wings and spreading their tails. At nesting time pairs of Galahs make their homes in tree hollows.

Hh Hopping-mouse

Hopping-mice are rodents, not marsupials, with long back legs for hopping. They live in the desert regions of Australia and avoid the heat of the day by resting in chambers about a metre below the surface where the sand is moist and cool. At night they emerge from tunnels to feed on insects and the seeds of spinifex and other grasses. Their nests have several entrances so they can quickly escape if a lizard or snake comes down their burrow. Hopping-mice receive all the water they need from their food.

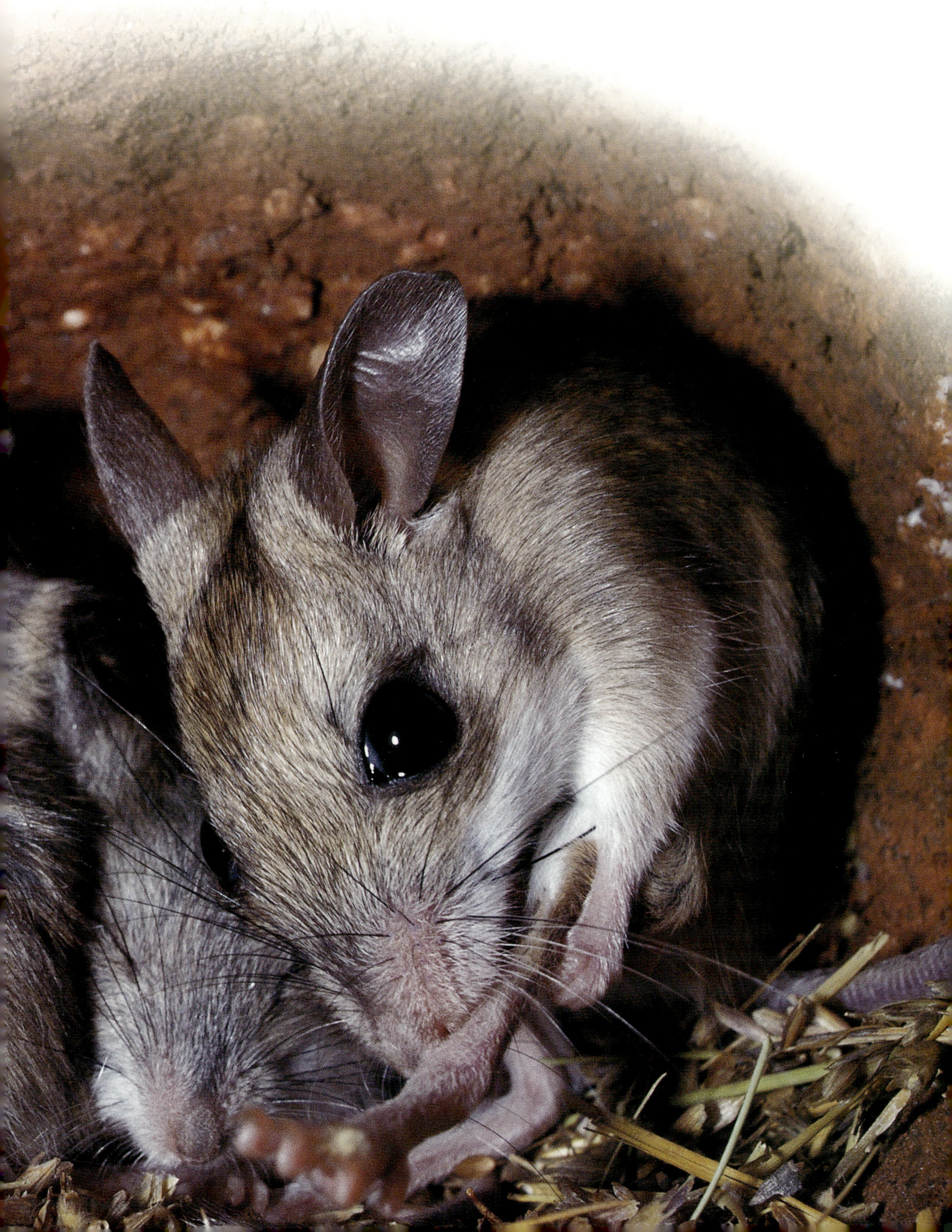

Ibis

The Sacred Ibis is found in most wetland areas of coastal Australia. It gathers in large flocks near lagoons and swamps, and can often be seen walking slowly across the mudflats or newly ploughed paddocks, jabbing and pushing its long curved bill into the soft wet earth for small creatures such as fish, frogs, worms and beetles. During breeding time hundreds, and sometimes thousands, of Sacred Ibis nest in groups, building their rough stick nests close together in trees and bushes in or near marshy water.

Jj Jabiru

The Jabiru is Australia's only stork. Sometimes called the Black-neck Stork, it is a large bird measuring 1.5 metres, with a beautiful shiny blue-green neck. It inhabits the coastal and inland wetlands of tropical northern and eastern Australia, where it forages for fish, frogs, insects and worms. During the breeding season the Jabiru builds a rough platform of sticks, rushes and grass in a tree – sometimes as high as 25 metres above ground – where it lays between two to four eggs.

Kk Kangaroo

The Red Kangaroo, is the largest of the Australian kangaroos and is widespread across the whole of the country, except the far north, mountainous east coast, and southern coastal regions. Kangaroos graze on grass and the leaves of shrubs and trees in the early morning and evening, and at night. They rest during the day. The young kangaroo is born without fur and weighs less than a gram. It crawls through the mother's fur to attach itself to one of the teats in the forward opening pouch.

Koala

The Koala is a marsupial, not a bear. It lives in trees, coming down to the ground to move from tree to tree. It is a solitary animal, feeding mostly at night, and sleeping during the day. Koalas can eat only the leaves of a few smooth barked gum trees which are low in tannin and essential oils. The female Koala has one young which she carries in a backward opening pouch for up to six months and then on her back for up to three months. Koalas are found throughout South Australia, Victoria, New South Wales and Queensland.

Ll Lorikeet

Lorikeets are parrots, with tongues especially equipped with brush-tips to feed on the nectar and pollen of flowering gums and other native trees. The Purple-crowned Lorikeet is smaller than a Budgerigar, and at first glance, does not look very colourful. It has a few small patches of colour on its head, but it is only when it flies that its bright red underwings are exposed. Flocks of Purple-crowned Lorikeets live in the forests and woodlands of southern Australia. They nest in tree hollows where they lay three to four eggs.

Mm

Magpie

Magpies are distinctive black and white birds with long sharp beaks that are found in most of Australia, except deserts and rainforests. They are well known for their rich carolling song, which is often given in chorus with other members of the group. They live in family flocks rather than pairs, and guard their territory vigorously. From August to October Magpies build large untidy nests high up in trees with sticks and occasional pieces of wire and plastic. The female lays two to five eggs. All Magpies have a strong instinct to defend their chicks by swooping on anything that approaches their nests.

Nn Numbat

The Australian Numbat is most beautifully coloured. Its fur grades from red at the head to black on the back, and is striped white. Its tail is long and bushy. The Numbat feasts on termites, scratching in soil and rotting wood to find the termite tunnels below, and licking them up with its long, sticky tongue. Numbats are active during the day but have extremely good hearing, and are quick to retreat to a hollow log for safety. They are found only in south-west Australia.

Oo

Owl

The Barking Owl gets its name from its quick double hoot that sounds like the bark of a dog. The call varies from a clear *wook-wook* to a soft *wuff-wuff* and is used mostly at night when the Barking Owl hunts for insects, birds and small mammals, such as rabbits. During the day it roosts high up in the dense foliage of a tall tree. The Barking Owl is found in woodland areas across northern Australia. It nests in a large tree hollow, and lays two to three white eggs.

Pp

Possum

The Honey Possum is a tiny, mouse-sized marsupial with a slender snout and a long brush-tipped tongue for poking down flowers in search of pollen and nectar. Honey Possums feed at night on nectar-producing banksias, bottlebrushes, and other wildflowers found only in south-west Western Australia. The female gives birth to two to four babies weighing less than 5 milligrams, which she carries in a pouch.

Parrot

The Turquoise Parrot is a small colourful parrot found in south-eastern Australia. It feeds in flocks or pairs on the ground, where it searches for the seeds of grasses and other plants. Turquoise Parrots live in open woodlands and farmland. They make their nests in small hollows - quite often in tree stumps and fence posts - close to the ground. The male feeds the female while she waits for her eggs to hatch.

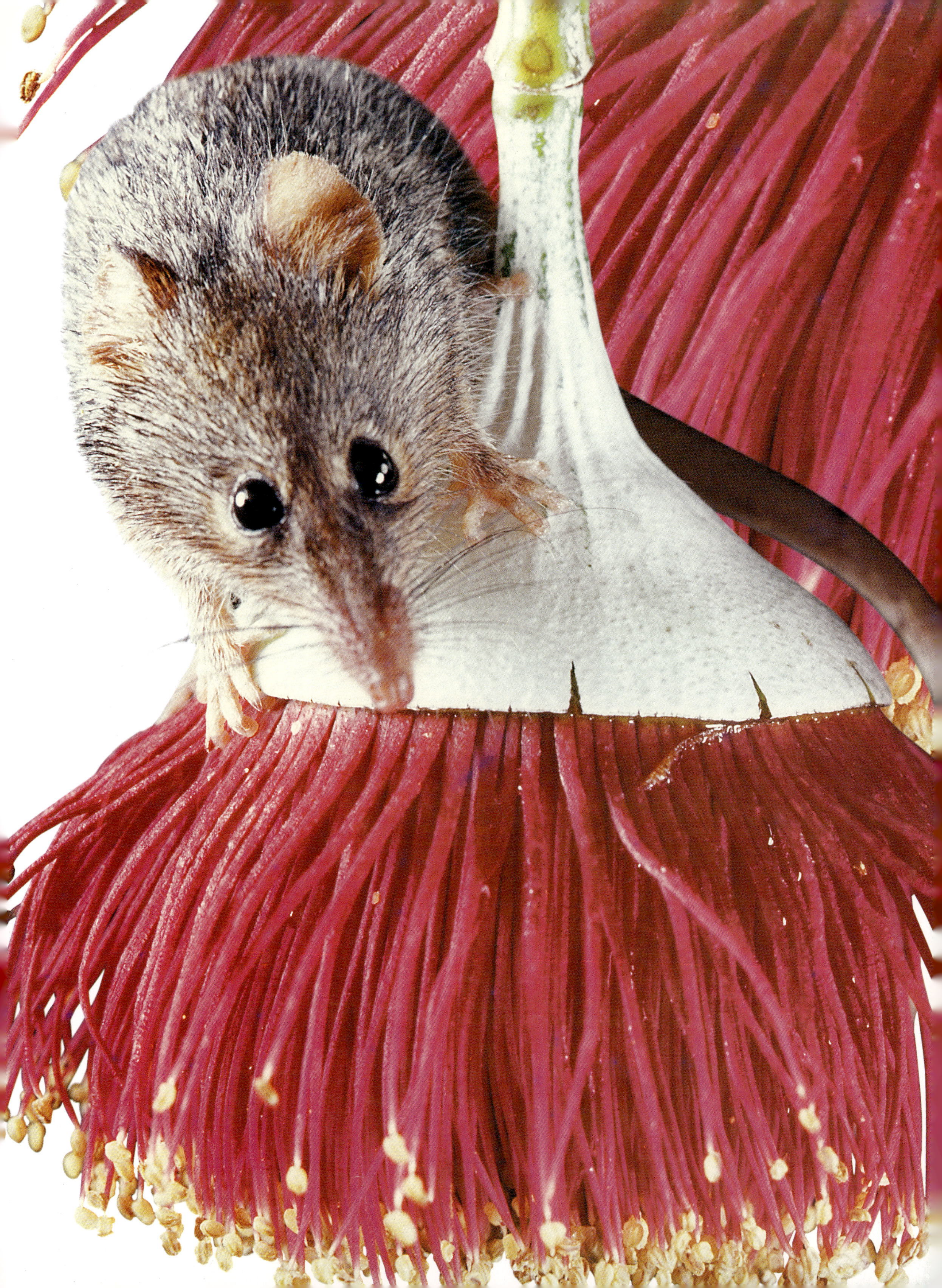

Qq Quoll

The Northern Quoll is a medium-sized marsupial that is easily identified by its white spots and bushy tail. It is a fierce meat-eater with a fine, pointed snout and a mouth full of needle-sharp teeth. It lives in dens among rocks and boulders or in the hollows of trees, and hunts at night. Among its prey are rock-rats, Antechinuses, small reptiles and insects. The female has up to eight babies which she carries clinging to her fur for approximately nine weeks. Northern Quolls are found in most parts of tropical northern Australia.

Rr

Rosella

The Crimson Rosella is one of the most common parrots of eastern Australia, and can be found in tropical rainforests as far north as Queensland and cool temperate forests as far south as Victoria. Though most at home in eucalypt areas, Crimson Rosellas feed on a wide range of exotic and native seeds and fruit, both on the ground and in the trees. Breeding adults nest in tree hollows. The female lays five to eight eggs, and is fed by the male while she waits for them to hatch.

Ss Spoonbill

The Yellow-billed Spoonbill is a common sight throughout most of Australia as it wades majestically along shallow stretches of inland and coastal water, in search of molluscs, fish and other water life. It feeds by swaying its bill from side to side in water and sand and sifting its catch through toothlike knobs on the end of its "spoon".

During breeding season Yellow-billed Spoonbills develop long white plumes on their necks and breasts. They nest in groups, building platforms of sticks in trees, bushes and reeds in or near water. Both adults take turns hatching up to four eggs.

Tt Tortoise

Unlike sea turtles, which have flippers, Australian Tortoises have webbed feet and claws. They live in swamps, lakes and rivers and come out on dry land to dig a hole and lay their eggs. They can also walk overland for short distances between waterholes. The Tortoise pictured here is known only by its Latin name, *Emydura victoriae*, and is found in the remote Kimberley region of north-west Australia. It eats what is available, including insects, larvae and other water creatures, as well as plants, small reptiles and even baby water birds.

Uu Ulysses Butterfly

With its wingspan of more than 12 centimetres and its vivid blue colour, the Ulysses Butterfly is the largest and most magnificent of all Australian butterflies. It is found only in the rainforests of north-eastern Queensland where it flits from one sunny spot to another, feeding on the long, tubular pink flowers of the native *Euodia* plant. After mating, the female lays her eggs on the leaves of this same plant. These leaves are later eaten by the tiny caterpillars when they hatch.

Vv Variegated Fairy Wren

The Variegated Fairy-wren is one of four species of chestnut-shouldered wrens, so named because they have a rusty red patch on each wing. Variegated Fairy-wrens are found throughout most of Australia, particularly the drier northern areas. They prefer dense, undisturbed vegetation and have a high pitched reeling trill. All fairy-wrens build a grass nest with a roof and an entrance at the side. They usually nest quite low, in a small bush or clump of grass. They lay between two to four speckled eggs.

Ww Wombat

Wombats are closely related to Koalas. There are two main types of wombat, the Common Wombat and the Hairy-nosed Wombat. The Hairy-nosed Wombat is distinguished from the Common Wombat by the fine, downy hairs on its nose, its soft, silky fur and its slightly longer ears. Wombats grow about a metre long and can weigh up to 30 kilograms. They live in deep burrows which often contain a number of large chambers and tunnels with several entrances. Wombats sleep during the day and come out at night to graze.

Wallaby

The Agile Wallaby has bright sandy or golden-brown fur with very distinct hip and cheek stripes, and short ears. It stands about 1 metre high, and has a tail a few centimetres shorter. It is found throughout the entire north of Australia, and is most often seen on coastal and river flood plains, where tropical grasses grow fast and tall after the summer wet season. Agile Wallabies often travel in groups of up to several hundred, feeding at night and sheltering during the day in patches of monsoonal jungle and dense scrub.

Xx eXtinct

When any living thing becomes so rare that it cannot be found, it is said to be extinct. The little marsupial Dibbler pictured here, was thought to be extinct for eighty-three years. No bigger than an ordinary house mouse, scientists believed it had been eaten by foxes and cats, or burnt out in bushfires. In 1967, however, a miraculous discovery was made when several Dibblers were caught in little cage traps set among the Banksia flowers near Albany in Western Australia. The Dibbler has since been found in a few other places, and is now protected, so that it cannot become "extinct" again!

Yy

Yellow-bellied Sunbird

The Yellow-bellied Sunbird lives on the edge of the rainforests and among the mangroves of coastal north-east Queensland, and is often seen darting among the foliage catching insects or hovering in front of a flower as it draws in nectar with its long downcurved bill. The Sunbird's nest is a domed structure, made of bark, leaves and cobwebs, with a side entrance. It hangs from a branch at its top, and has a long whip-like tail at its base. The female lays two to three speckled eggs.

Zz Zebra Finch

The Zebra Finch, so named because of its distinctive black and striped tail, is very common throughout the drier inland regions of Australia. It lives in open grassy country including farmlands, and is often seen in large flocks, especially when coming in to water. Finches feed on grass seeds and insects and must drink regularly from rivers, dams and water tanks. The Zebra Finch often choses a dense, prickly shrub to build its rough domed nest with a side entrance. The female lays three to seven eggs.